Hymns for All Seasons

Piano Settings by Jan Sanborn

Welcome to "Hymns for All Seasons." Although we customarily divide our days into winter-spring-summer-fall, in this collection I also have taken into consideration the major seasons of the church year, with settings of well-known Lent/Easter and Advent/Christmas hymns. Applicable, too, are these hymns to the seasons of our lives, as we daily walk with God enjoying all His gifts to us.

These arrangements are designed to help you with preludes, offertories and postludes. The table of contents is only a suggestion. Don't feel, for instance, that you are limited to playing "In the Garden" only in the month of June! May I also suggest that you expand some of my ideas to include an instrument or two to some of the settings? A flute with "Christ the Lord Is Risen Today," or string bass with "What Child Is This?" are a couple of possibilities.

Should you want to hear my own interpretation of these arrangements, a CD is available. I hope you'll enjoy playing them.

Jan Sanborn

for Roz Anderson

FOR THE BEAUTY OF THE EARTH

CONRAD KOCHER
Arranged by JAN SANBORN

17
dim. e rall.
a tempo
mf
21
pp
rall.
mp a tempo
25
cresc.
f
mp
29
rit.
f a tempo
33

37
ff
40
43
p
mf
Mel.
46
Slower
rall.
mp
49
p
pp
R.H.

for Kurt Kaiser

LOVE DIVINE, ALL LOVES EXCELLING

JOHN ZUNDEL
Arranged by JAN SANBORN

17
Mel.
mp a tempo
21
p
25
pp
rall.
29
mf piu mosso
32
cresc. poco a poco

35
38
41
mf
rall.
Tempo I
44
rall.
47
p
8vb

for Ty Osborn

THE OLD RUGGED CROSS

GEORGE BENNARD
Arranged by JAN SANBORN

21
ten.
mf
rall.
mp
25
a tempo
29
cresc.
33
mf
37
mp
p

41
mp
45
rall.
mf
a tempo
49
53
cresc. poco a poco
57
f

61
ten.
rall.
pp
a tempo
65
69
cresc.
mf
3
73
f
mf
77
rit.
p a tempo
rall.
81
8vb

for Rhoda Harrison Tuit

CHRIST THE LORD IS RISEN TODAY

LYRA DAVIDICA
Arranged by JAN SANBORN

26
f
31
Lightly, accented
mp
36
mf
41
mp
mf
46
f

p
ff
rit.

for Mark Thallander

MORNING PRAISE

Arranged by JAN SANBORN

15
8va
8va
ff
mp
8vb
19
Flowing
22
25
28
poco rit.

"Praise Him, All Ye Little Children"
(Carey Bonner)

"Alleluia"
(Wolfgang Amadeus Mozart)
Sweetly
p

63
mf
f
rit.
sub.p
♩ = 108
pp
67
simile
71
cresc. poco a poco
75
molto cresc. e rit.
ff
Tempo I
80
molto rit.

for Dick Bolks

IN THE GARDEN

C. AUSTIN MILES
Arranged by JAN SANBORN

21
25
L.H.
mf
R.H.
29
p
L.H.
simile
33
accel.
rall.
37
accel.
rit.

41
mp a tempo
Pedal lightly
45
49
53
rall.
57
Broaden
f
Tempo I
8va
mf

61
(8va)
f
65
(8va)
dim.
loco
p
69
ten.
rall.
ten.
8vb
73
rall.
77
a tempo
rit.
pp

for Dr. Kimo Smith

PROMISED LAND

TRADITIONAL AMERICAN MELODY
Arranged by JAN SANBORN

17
p
mp
21
mf
mf
24
27
31
dim. poco a poco

34
mp
pp
37
40
sfz
f
43
46

49
cresc.
52
rall.
ff a tempo
55
mf cresc.
58
molto rit.
ff
f a tempo
61
L.H.

for Carol Hughes

HE LEADETH ME

WILLIAM B. BRADBURY
Arranged by JAN SANBORN

17
rall.
21
a tempo
26
cresc. poco a poco
31
f
dim.
mf
36
piu mosso

41
rall.
46
a tempo
cresc.
f
51
molto rit.
p
a tempo
56
60
pp
8vb
8vb

for Lois Bock

GIVE ME JESUS

TRADITIONAL SPIRITUAL
Arranged by JAN SANBORN

Freely, with conviction **(♩ = 72)**

13
piu mosso
16
rall.
a tempo
19
p
22
Tempo I
rall.
cresc. poco a poco
25

29
f
rall.
pp
a tempo
32
cresc. poco a poco
35
f
38
dim. poco a poco
41
rit.

for Dr. Ken Mays

THE CHURCH'S ONE FOUNDATION

SAMUEL S. WESLEY
Arranged by JAN SANBORN

Rhythmically, assertively (♩ = 104)

16
f
20
mp
Mel.
24
R.H.
28
31
p
legato

34
37
pp
40
cresc. poco a poco
43
Broadly
rall.
ff
46

49
52
p
55
♩ = 100
ff
58
61
rit.

for Allan Petker

LET ALL THINGS NOW LIVING

TRADITIONAL WELSH MELODY
Arranged by JAN SANBORN

Lightly, spirited (♩ = 132)

21
cresc. poco a poco
p
f
mf Mel.
25
29
Mel.
mp
33
mf
37
cresc. poco a poco
f
mf
41

45
cresc.
f
sub.p
49
53
mf
57
simile
61
cresc.
f
65

69
p
8vb
73
cresc. poco a poco
rall.
Broadly
77
ff
81
85
no rit.

for Bryan Jeffery Leech

ONCE IN ROYAL DAVID'S CITY

HENRY J. GAUNTLETT
Arranged by JAN SANBORN

17
p
simile
mf
21
mp
cresc. poco a poco
mf
24
rall.
R.H.
pp a tempo
27
30
f

32
34
36
dim. e rall.
38
Slower, pensively
p
mp
41
rit.
L.H.

for Edie Lehmann Boddicker

WHAT CHILD IS THIS?

TRADITIONAL ENGLISH MELODY
Arranged by JAN SANBORN

19
24
29
cresc.
rall.
mf a tempo
34
cresc. poco a poco
39
rall.
f a tempo

44
49
54
dim. poco a poco
pp
rall.
59
a tempo
64
rit.
R.H.

for Dr. Duane Funderburk

ANGELS WE HAVE HEARD ON HIGH

TRADITIONAL FRENCH MELODY
Arranged by JAN SANBORN

Rollicking, accented (♩ = 144)

21
sfz
f
mf
25
p cresc. poco a poco
29
f
L.H.
33
37
pp
41
cresc. poco a poco

45
f
molto rit.
49
ff a tempo
53
l'istesso
57
l'istesso
61
sfz
sfz
65
sfz

Jan Sanborn *is a pianist of great flexibility and creativity. She began her piano studies at the age of three, and by the age of six she was the pianist for her local church. She studied at Iowa State University, Drake University, Westmont College and California State University Northridge, where she is now staff accompanist.*

As an accompanist-arranger, Jan traveled with the Roger Wagner Chorale on a number of their Far East tours, and performed with the Pacific and Angeles Chorales in Southern California. She appears as a regular guest artist with the Los Angeles Chamber Singers, both in concert and recording.

As a composer she has written many anthems for choirs and keyboard books. She serves on the editorial board of the Fred Bock Music Companies, and is a longtime member of ASCAP.

Fred Bock Music Company